Darw… Discovery

by Jillian Powell

Contents

Map of Darwin's voyage

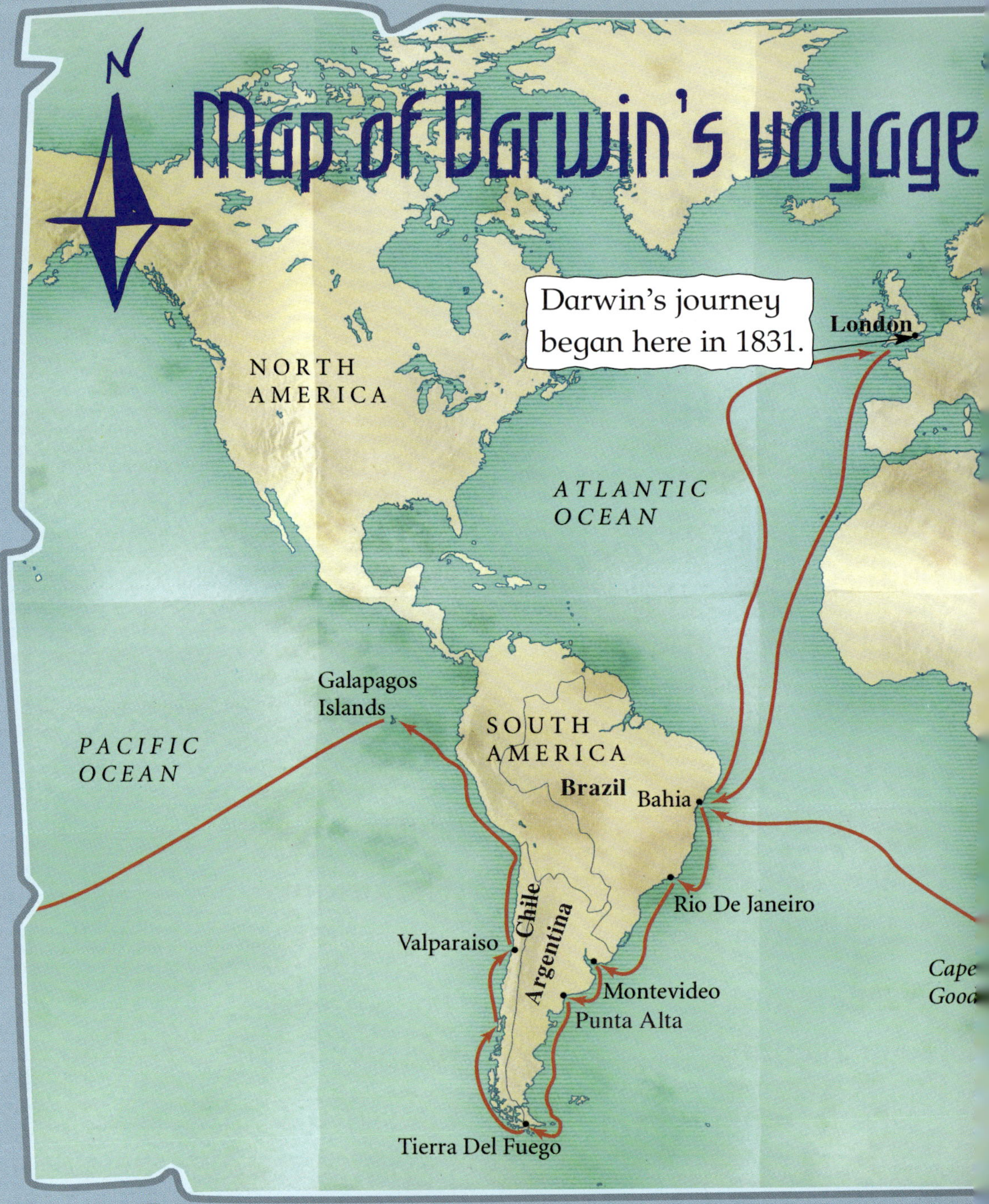

PE
ASIA
RICA
INDIAN OCEAN
Mauritius
AUSTRALIA
PACIFIC OCEAN
N
W
E
S
SOUTHERN OCEAN
NEW ZEALAND

A voyage of discovery

Charles Darwin was twenty-two years old when he was offered the chance of a lifetime. A **survey** ship called HMS *Beagle* was setting sail on a voyage round the world. Its captain was Robert FitzRoy. He was looking for someone to come on the voyage to collect plants, animals, rocks and minerals from all the countries they visited.

Darwin loved **natural history**. He had collected plants and insects since he was a little boy. When he was a student, he began to study rocks and fossils. By travelling with Captain FitzRoy, he could travel round the world, discovering wonderful new plants and creatures.

The voyage of HMS *Beagle* would be an amazing adventure. The ship would visit high mountains, rainforests and tropical islands. The journey round the world would last five years.

HMS Beagle

HMS *Beagle* was a Royal Navy survey ship. The Royal Navy used survey ships to make maps of the seas and to collect information about the world. The main reason for HMS *Beagle's* voyage was to survey the coasts of Central and South America, and groups of Pacific islands.

The ship was just under thirty metres long, built of wood and copper plates. It had three masts and was fitted out as a warship with sixteen cannons on board. Smaller boats were tied to the decks. These were used to ferry people and supplies ashore and to explore rivers inland.

There were seventy-five people on board. They included ship's officers and seamen, carpenters, sailmakers, cooks and a **surgeon**. There was also a ship's artist, three passengers and Darwin.

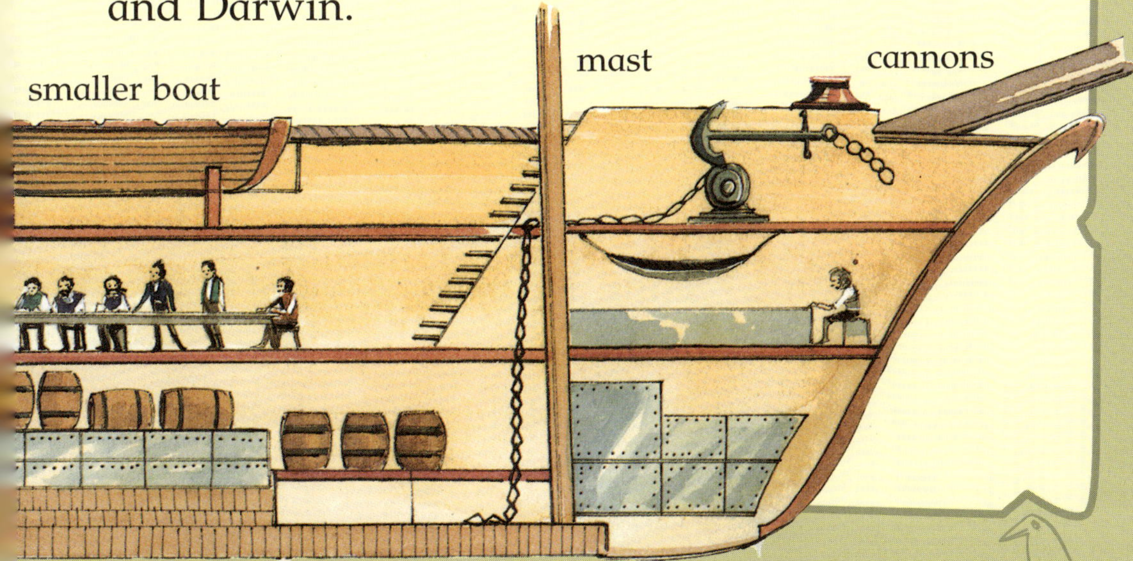

HMS Beagle sets sail

HMS *Beagle* set sail from Plymouth on 27 December 1831.

Darwin travelled as an unpaid passenger. He shared a tiny cabin with the ship's Chief Surveyor. It was so small that when he went to bed, Darwin had to take out a drawer from a chest to make room for his feet.

For the first few weeks, he was very seasick and ate only raisins. He spent most of his time resting in his hammock, and reading the latest scientific books. After a few weeks he got used to the rocking of the ship.

He began collecting **specimens** of sea creatures, by rigging up a net to tow behind the ship. The sailors laughed and complained about the mess he made on deck.

February 1832

"I loathe, I abhor the sea and all the ships which sail on it. Not even the thrill of geology makes up for the misery and vexation that comes with seasickness."

On 28 February 1832, after sixty-three days at sea, HMS *Beagle* landed at San Salvador, Brazil.

loathe: hate
abhor: detest
vexation: pain and grief

The Brazilian rainforest

The next day, Darwin went ashore to explore the Brazilian rainforest and collect specimens. He was amazed by the colourful flowers and strange plants growing in the rainforest. He noted how well plants had adapted to the heat and rain of the forest. They had big glossy leaves that let the rain run off them easily.

He saw orange, mango and banana trees, coconuts and palms. He had to shelter under a tree when he got caught in a tropical storm, and he noted how the rain was so heavy that it ran down the tree trunk in torrents.

He was also fascinated by the insects, which included huge, brightly coloured butterflies. One day, he watched a spider fighting a wasp. After a struggle, the wasp killed the spider. Darwin collected both of them as specimens.

29 February 1832

"The noise of the insects is so loud, that it may be heard even in a vessel anchored several yards from the shore."

vessel: boat

Darwin's job

Darwin collected plants, animals, insects, birds, rocks and fossils. Every day, he kept a diary and a journal in which he listed all his discoveries.

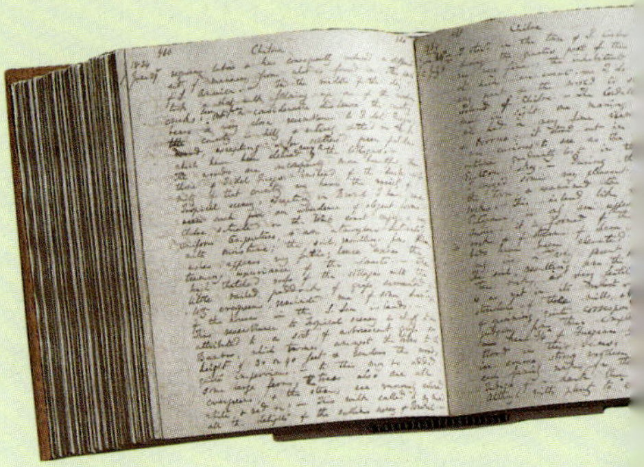

Darwin's journal

First he had to find, trap or shoot his specimens. Then he had to preserve them. Some had to be wrapped and others had to be bottled. Some animals were skinned, and others dried and stuffed with straw.

Darwin carefully labelled each specimen, and wrote notes about them. He then put them in special metal boxes, and packed them into barrels to be sent back by ship to London, where scientists could study them.

He sent back stuffed birds and mice, bags of plant seed, fish pickled in jars, and insects wrapped in cotton wool.

The giants' graveyard

Darwin's journey from Brazil to Argentina.

In 1833, HMS *Beagle* sailed south from Brazil to the coast of Argentina. At a place called Punta Alta, Darwin found hundreds of fossils and animal bones in the cliffs and on the beach. There were huge skeletons of animals that had become **extinct**.

Darwin found the head of a giant sloth called a Megatherium.

The beach was a giants' graveyard. Darwin took all the fossils and bones back on to the deck of HMS *Beagle*. They made him wonder why animals became extinct.

August 1833

"In the gravel a considerable number of bones were embedded … first, a tolerably perfect head of a megatherium, and a fragment and teeth of two others; second, an animal of the order Edentata, as large as a pony, and with great scratching claws."

A model made from the bones of a gigantic capybara. It looked like a cross between a rat and a hippopotamus.

considerable number: quite a lot
tolerably: fairly
fragment: a small piece
of the order: belonging to the group

Native peoples

Darwin's journey from Argentina to Tierra del Fuego.

HMS *Beagle* travelled south towards the tip of South America. By summer, it had reached Tierra del Fuego, where it anchored for a few days to let some passengers go ashore. On a previous sea voyage, Captain FitzRoy had taken a few of the native people back to England to be educated. Now three of them were going home.

Sketches of the three passengers.

There were two men and a woman. In England, they had become Christians and learned to speak English, as well as skills like gardening. The islands off Cape Horn where they lived were cold and windy, and Darwin was surprised to see the simple life their people lived.

They slept in huts and wore clothes made from animal skins. They still used stone tools and ate wild animals and berries.

Rocks and landforms

HMS *Beagle* spent some time surveying the coast of Argentina. Then in 1834, it sailed round Cape Horn and reached the Pacific Ocean. It then sailed north along the coast of Chile. Darwin went ashore to study the **landforms**, and to collect rocks and fossils.

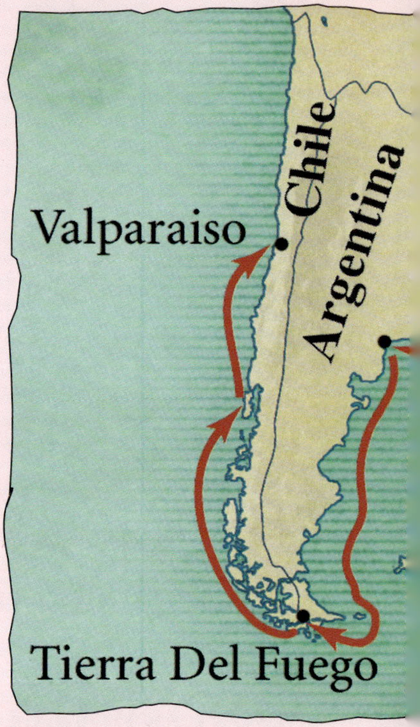

Darwin's journey from Tierra del Fuego round Cape Horn to Chile.

Examples of fossils.

Darwin rode on a mule up into the Andes mountains. When he was 4000 metres above sea-level, he found fossils of sea creatures in the rocks. From this evidence Darwin knew that the rocks he was standing on must once have been in the sea.

He was beginning to realise that the rocks were much older than people thought. Over millions of years, they had been shaped and changed by natural forces like earthquakes and volcanoes.

The rocks were once under the sea.

Natural forces forced rocks above sea-level.

The Galapagos Islands

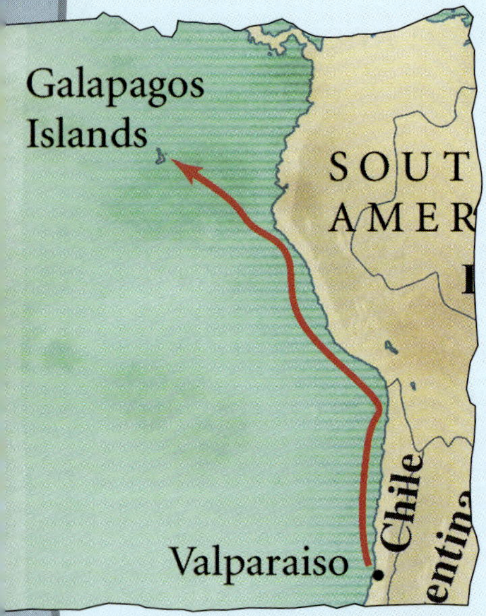

Darwin's journey from Chile to the Galapagos Islands.

HMS *Beagle* headed up the west coast of South America towards the Galapagos Islands, or islas galápagos in Spanish (islas means islands and galápagos means tortoises). On 15 September 1835 the ship landed and Darwin went ashore.

The islands were strange and exciting. They had been formed by underwater volcanoes and had black rocky valleys where cactus plants grew.

The ship's crew found giant tortoises there, and rode them like horses. There were many other strange creatures like iguanas, which looked like huge lizards, and lots of different types of birds.

Darwin noticed that each island had its own plants, birds and animals. Local people knew which island a tortoise came from by the shape of its shell. The islands made Darwin begin to wonder how all these plants and animals had **evolved**.

29 September 1835

"The rocks on the coast abounded with great black lizards between three and four feet long; and on the hills, another species was equally common."

abounded: covered with

Finches

Darwin was especially interested in one group of birds, the finches. There were thirteen different **species** of finch on the Galapagos Islands and none was found anywhere else in the world. They were all small and brown, green or black, but Darwin noticed that each species had a different–shaped beak. Darwin believed that some finches must have been blown to the Galapagos Islands by storms. Over many years, the birds' beaks had changed to suit the food they found to eat on each island.

Some finches had strong beaks for crushing tough seeds.

Some had small beaks for cracking open small hard seeds.

Others had long pointed beaks for finding insects in the cracks of rocks or tree bark.

Others had sharp curved beaks for eating buds and leaves.

Darwin's discoveries

Darwin made lots of notes and drawings in his journal. He began thinking about how all the different creatures on the Galapagos Islands had arrived there. Birds, insects and seeds could have been blown by the wind from the mainland. Bigger creatures like the tortoises had probably floated there on rafts of plant roots and leaves.

Darwin worked out that all the different creatures had evolved so they would find food and survive on the islands.

As well as specimens in tins and jars, Darwin had lots of new ideas to take home with him.

HMS *Beagle* left the Galapagos Islands on 20 October 1835. It crossed the Pacific Ocean to reach New Zealand and Australia. Then it sailed across the Indian Ocean, round the Cape of Good Hope, and back to Brazil, before finally setting off for home.

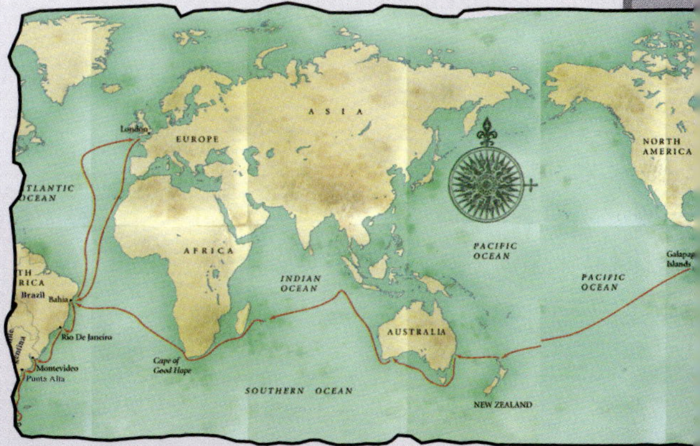

Darwin's journey from the Galapagos Islands to New Zealand and Australia, Brazil and then back home.

Darwin's theory

HMS *Beagle* arrived home from the voyage on 2 October 1836. The journey had covered over 60,000 kilometres and lasted nearly five years. Once home, Darwin began to use all his notes and ideas to work on a theory of **evolution**.

The Bible taught that everything on Earth had been created by God in seven days. Many people believed the Creation took place around 4000 BC.

But Darwin's study of rocks and fossils taught him that the Earth was many millions of years old. He also realised that different species of animals and plants had evolved over millions of years.

The ones that adapted best had survived. But others had become extinct.

Some of the jars containing the specimens which Darwin sent home.

October 1836

"On the 25th we called at the island of St Michael's for letters, and then steered a direct course for England. On October 2nd the Beagle anchored at Falmouth, where I left her, having lived on board the little vessel very nearly five years."

The origin of species

Darwin worked on his **theory** for over twenty years. Then in November 1859, he published his book *On the Origin of Species*. He used all the scientific evidence he had found on his voyage to show that the Earth was millions of years old, and that life had evolved over the years.

In his book, Darwin explained that all animals and plants change with time, and nature chooses which ones survive. He called this **natural selection**. His theory is based on the idea that all living things have to struggle to find food, living space and mates. Some features will help them survive, such as animals developing sharp teeth to help them hunt, or plants producing more seeds that will grow into new plants. The creatures which survive are the ones best suited to their surroundings.

The spread of Darwinism

People made fun of Darwin.

At first, many people thought Darwin's ideas were crazy. Religious people were angry that Darwin was questioning God's Creation. But some scientists read Darwin's work and believed that he had made an important discovery. They examined all the evidence from his voyage, like the fossils and bones of extinct animals, and his studies of the different species that had evolved on the Galapagos Islands. They agreed that Darwin's voyage on HMS *Beagle* had been a true voyage of discovery.

Darwin's voyage was so important to science that the ***Beagle 2*** *space probe to Mars was named after it.*

Glossary

evolution: the process of development from earlier forms

evolve: to develop from earlier forms

extinct: no longer existing

landform: a form or feature of the landscape

natural history: the study of nature and living things

natural selection: the way nature selects which species survive and which die out

species: a class of living things which are alike

specimen: an example or sample of something

surgeon: a doctor who performs operations

survey: a detailed study

theory: a view of something based on study and research

Index